CREATING JOYFUL MEMORIES FO PEOPLE WITH MEMORY LOSS

- **PLAN** to spend time with your friend during the hours that best fit into his regular routine.
- **KEEP TRIPS OR ACTIVITIES** as simple as possible, giving instructions one at a time.
- **WHEN PLANS CHANGE,** be flexible, allowin the person to lead whenever possible.
- **PROVIDE** memory aides such as signs, maps, videos, and photos. Take along a camera; then head with your friend to a familiar place and see what develops!
- **ASK** about the person's hobbies, interests, and lifestyle as a conversation starter. If she loves books or movies, plan to enjoy them together and fill in the parts where she might get confused.
- **BE GENTLE** and supportive when a friend appears to struggle with a location or concept.
- **GET MOVING**—swim, bike, dance with friends. Remember, however, that sitting and listening to music can also be as comforting as these other more "active" pastimes.
- **ASK** primary caregivers how you can assist them with tasks, or how you can provide them with respite time to recharge.

---

[6] *Second Forgetting: Remembering the Power of the Gospel during Alzheimer's Disease* (Grand Rapids, MI: Zondervan, 2014): p. 79.

[7] From "2016 Alzheimer's Disease Facts and Figures," published by the Alzheimer's Associatior and available online at http://www.alz.org/facts/overview.asp

[8] J. Robertson McQuilkin, *Living By Vows* (Columbia, SC: Columbia International University, 1995).

What NOT to Do…

- **DON'T TAKE** the person's behaviors personally, since these can vary from day to day.
- **DON'T TRY** to fill in missing words in his conversation unless he encourages you to do so.
- **DON'T ALLOW** yourself or your friend to become overly tired during an activity; take frequent breaks.
- **DON'T RAISE** your voice or scold the person—the disease, not the person, is the problem.
- **DON'T ARGUE** or try to "reason" with the person—go along with her way of thinking.
- **DON'T BE DISCOURAGED** if you fail to see progress in your relationship. Your friendship is important and is being used by God.
- **DON'T LEAVE** a person with memory loss alone in a store, restaurant, or car. Some are wanderers.

"Marge and I were always so excited when the spring seed catalogs came in the mail. Long before planting season, we would lay out our shared garden space and order seeds. When Marge's dementia began, we determined that nothing would change–but eventually, it did. For the next eight years, we planted fewer and fewer vegetables, and I did more of the work. The pride in Marge's eyes…and mine, however, remained the same until our final goodbye."

–SOPHIE, A TRUE FRIEND TO MARGE

2. Moderate Alzheimer's Disease (middle-stage)

- **THINGS** that happened years ago become more real than current daily activities. Conversations include loved ones who passed away years earlier.
- **PAPERWORK** becomes nearly impossible due to a forgotten address, date of birth or phone number; the person is no longer able to manage finances.
- **DAYS AND NIGHTS** get mixed up, causing changes in sleeping and eating habits.
- **INCREASED SUPERVISION** is required because the person can get lost, even in favorite places.
- **CONFUSION** can lead to depression, mistrust, and fear that personal items are being stolen.
- **AS THE INDIVIDUAL'S GRASP** of reality fades, personality changes result in a greater loss of independence and can prove challenging for caregivers.

"Frustrated? Yes! I'm the sole caregiver for my wife who has Alzheimer's. Here are just some of the things she experiences almost daily. She can't find her clothes and won't believe that she is in her own house. She thinks that I'm lying to her and doesn't know we are married. She won't believe that her parents are dead. She doesn't remember that she just had lunch and wants to eat again. If I let her out of my sight, she walks down the street, trying to go home. I try to control my frustration in positive ways. It helps to trust that God has everything under control and is working in our best interest."

—HAL, HUSBAND OF JO, A CHURCH OFFICE MANAGER

. Mild Alzheimer's Disease (early-stage)

- **LIFE** seems to go on as usual with work, driving, shopping, and social activities.
- **REMEMBERING THINGS** like appointments, birthdays, familiar objects, or words becomes difficult.
- **PROBLEM-SOLVING** and organizational skills seem unfocused, causing further distractions.
- **READING,** using a computer, and even watching television can be frustrating due to forgotten passwords or story lines.
- **ASK THE PERSON** to draw a clock face with hands pointing to a specific time. As the disease progresses, the resulting drawing will become increasingly distorted.

"Our son spent a week's vacation with us. He and his dad enjoyed their usual fishing trip, car shows, and ball games. At the end of the week, our son came to me and said, 'Mom, there is something wrong with dad.' I told him that his father's allergies were acting up and he was struggling with a new computer program at the office. But he said, 'No, Mom! There is something wrong with dad.' That day I began to keep a list of my husband's behaviors that did seem odd. Six months later, he was diagnosed with the early stages of Alzheimer's."

—LYNN, WIFE OF RICHARD, A BASS FISHERMAN

MEMORY LOSS IMPACTS THE WHOLE FAMILY

"I am the good shepherd; I know my own sheep, and they know me."

—JOHN 10:14

JESUS IS the gatekeeper of our lives, including our minds. And we are so much more than simply our memories—even when our cognitive abilities fade, his knowledge of and love for us never does. We can still know and recognize the "voice" of our Lord and Savior, the Good Shepherd. He knows each one of us personally, intimately, and by name—and nothing whatsoever, not even severe dementia or memory loss, can snatch us from his loving embrace.

Alzheimer's is like the thief who sneaks into a sheepfold to steal the sheep. But Jesus is "the one who enters through the gate…and the sheep recognize his voice and come to him…he walks ahead of them, and they follow him because they know his voice" (John 10:1–5).

Whether you've known someone with memory loss for years or whether you've just met, this person is deeply cherished by God, who is working out his perfect will—even when we don't understand.

"I still wonder why God chose to take my mom this way, but the silent visits I had with her gave me time to reflect on her relationship with the Lord over the years. And I slowed down long enough to examine my relationship with him too. My mom lived a good and faithful life, and she was a light to others

even as she lay there in the peace and quiet. I also believe God communicated with my mom in some way during those final weeks, because God's Spirit doesn't need us to be verbal in order to be in relationship with him."

—DONNA, DAUGHTER OF HELEN,
A SCHOOL CAFETERIA WORKER

"The hardest part of living with a loved one with Alzheimer's is the constant changes–not knowing what to expect next. Sometimes change comes slowly, and other times it comes in a crash course–like dominos tumbling rapidly downhill. For a long time, I thought that this disease was something happening to my sweet husbanc and I needed to help him. But as we got to the mid- and late-stage Alzheimer's, God made it so clear that this was also happening to me. It was intended for my own growth in grace and character. It's the changes that are deepening in me that I'm paying close attention to these days."[9]

–PAT, WIFE OF STAN
A RETIRED BOEING ENGINEE

[9] "Pat Verbal Interview," Joni and Friends Radio, Interview with Joni Eareckson Tada (November 13, 2013) http://www.joniandfriends.org/radio/5-minute/pat-verbal-interview/

ALZHEIMER'S IS A SLOWLY PROGRESSING DISEASE

THE AVERAGE LIFE expectancy of a person who has been diagnosed with Alzheimer's is about 8-10 years. It is hard to watch a friend or loved one deteriorate through the years. While symptoms can fade in and out, the stages of Alzheimer's bring progressive decline. "My mom went through some difficult times," says Melissa, "but other seasons were not as challenging. I compared it to motherhood. Having a newborn can really wear you out, but that stage is only for a short time. In a few months, things may be completely different. Take the stages one day at a time and trust God for patience and strength. I tried to savor the last days with my mom even though they were difficult ones, and I'm glad I did."

"We know what real love is because Jesus gave up his life for us. So we also ought to give up our lives for our brothers and sisters.... Let's not merely say that we love each other; let us show the truth by our actions."—1 JOHN 3:16, 18

It may be confusing when you see these signs, but often a friend with limited interaction can see what close family members might miss. If you do, begin by praying for the person and their family. Take enough time to be confident about your observations, and then choose an appropriate time and place to share your concerns with a member of the family. It is not necessary to offer advice. Simply share your concern and offer support.

While the onset of Alzheimer's strikes fear in our hearts, God is greater than our fears. A friend or loved one may forget our name, but God always remembers.

"Don't be afraid, for I am with you. Don't be discouraged, for I am your God. I will strengthen you and help you. I will hold you up with my victorious right hand."

—ISAIAH 41:10

"Do not be afraid, for I have ransomed you. I have called you by name; you are mine."

—ISAIAH 43:1

"I, the LORD, made you, and I will not forget you."

—ISAIAH 44:21

"Alzheimer's is a messy and inconvenient condition. And so, people with Alzheimer's are often messy and yes, a little inconvenient. But they are people; they have souls. And they are in there, and also in our communities and part of our families.... What a joy it is to bring God's healing touch to those the world casts aside."

–JONI EARECKSON TADA

TIPS FOR MINISTERING TO PEOPL[E] AFFECTED BY MEMORY LOSS

It has been said that Alzheimer's disease is like tearing out the pages of a favorite book, one page at a time. But as Christians we believe God's commands are in our hearts, helping us to do what is right[10]—and that includes supporting friends and families affected by memory loss. Here are some tips for getting involved in memory care ministry:

- **LEARN** about the needs of people with memory loss from organizations that raise awareness and donations for medical research. See "Resources" at the end of this brochure.
- **VOLUNTEER** at local memory-care homes where you can spend time improving the lives of those who don't have local family members.
- **OFFER MEMORY-LOSS SUPPORT** groups or adult day center programs at your church.
- **ASK CAREGIVERS** how you can support a family: bring in meals, run errands, and read to or take a walk with someone with Alzheimer's.
- **OFFER TO STAY** with a person who needs care so the whole family can attend church together.
- **CONSIDER** becoming a hospice volunteer to give support during the end-of-life stage.
- **PARTICIPATE** in a "Walk to End Alzheimer's" local event with your family and friends. See www.alz.org.

[10] Romans 2:14-15

Books

- ***A PROMISE KEPT,* BY ROBERTSON MCQUILKIN** (Carol Stream, IL: Tyndale House Publishers, 1998) is a true tale of love and devotion. McQuilkin, who resigned as president of Columbia International University to care for his wife with Alzheimer's, shares the story of their struggles and the remarkable lessons about God's love.
- ***SECOND FORGETTING: REMEMBERING THE POWER OF THE GOSPEL DURING ALZHEIMER'S DISEASE,* BY DR. BENJAMIN T. MAST** (Grand Rapids, MI: Zondervan, 2014) highlights the power of the gospel through the personal stories of families coping with Alzheimer's. Dr. Mast answers questions about the disease and its effects on personal identity and faith as he explores the biblical importance of remembering and God's commitment to not forget his people.
- ***WHAT'S HAPPENING TO GRANDPA?,* BY MARIA SHRIVER** (New York, NY: Little, Brown and Company and Warner Books, 2004) is a children's book written to help children better understand the effects of aging and illness, especially Alzheimer's.

FRIENDS ARE OFTEN "FIRST RESPONDERS"

You may be witnessing the early onset of Alzheimer's if...

- **YOUR CO-WORKER** starts to miss regularly scheduled meetings or forgets people's names.
- **YOUR "SHOP-TILL-YOU-DROP"** friend can't find her car in the parking lot, starts asking you to drive, and is making some unusual purchases.
- **THE LEADER** of your Bible study seems frustrated because he can't locate or quote favorite Scripture passages anymore.
- **YOUR NEIGHBOR'S** mailbox is full even though he's home, and it's unlike him to leave tools in the yard and the garage door open.
- **A COUPLE** you hang out with begins to avoid social events, church services, and game night.
- **OVER DINNER** at a friend's house, the host asks you the same question four times and brings you the wrong drink.
- **A SUPER-ORGANIZED TEAM PLAYER** suddenly can't follow a checklist or schedule.

While the odds of experiencing memory loss increase with age, fewer than 1 in 5 people over age 65 get Alzheimer's, and less than half of those over 85 have the disease.[4] Perhaps more disturbing is the growing number of younger adults who are diagnosed with dementia. According to the Alzheimer's Association, an estimated 200,000 people in the United States with busy families and careers have early-onset Alzheimer's in their 40s and 50s.[5] This makes it especially important to know the early signs of memory loss and be proactive in seeking professional help.

---

[1] Cassandra Vinograd, "Pat Summitt, Legendary Women's Basketball Coach, Dies at 64," NBC News (June 28, 2016) http://www.nbcnews.com/news/sports/pat-summitt-legendary-women-s-basketball-coach-dies-64-n600136

[2] Eleanor Clift and Evan Thomas, "How Nancy Reagan coped with Ronald Reagan's Alzheimer's Disease," Newsweek (March 7, 2016) http://www.newsweek.com/nancy-reagan-coped-ronald-reagans-alzheimers-disease-president-434187

[3] From "2016 Alzheimer's Disease Facts and Figures," published by the Alzheimer's Association and available online at http://www.alz.org/facts/overview.asp

[4] From American Psychological Association Fact Sheet on "Memory and Aging," http://www.apa.org/pi/aging/memory-and-aging.pdf

[5] "Younger/Early Onset Alzheimer's & Dementia," http://www.alz.org/alzheimers_disease_early_onset.asp

Online Resources

- **THE ALZHEIMER'S ASSOCIATION** advances research to end Alzheimer's and dementia while enhancing care for those living with the disease. www.alz.org
- **THE NATIONAL INSTITUTE ON AGING** is working to discover what may contribute to healthy old age as well as to understand and address the diseases and disabilities sometimes associated with growing older. www.nia.nih.gov/alzheimers
- **THE ALZHEIMER'S FOUNDATION OF AMERICA (AFA)** unites more than 2,400 member organizations dedicated to meeting the educational, social, emotional, and practical needs of individuals with Alzheimer's disease and related illnesses, as well as those of their caregivers and families. www.alzfdn.org
- **JONI AND FRIENDS, "PEOPLE WITH ALZHEIMER'S ARE STILL PEOPLE."** In honor of National Alzheimer's Disease Awareness Month, Joni Eareckson Tada's blog offers encouragement on connecting with friends with Alzheimer's, including a video demonstrating the power of human connection. www.joniandfriends.org/blog/people-with-alzheimers
- **THE CAREGIVER'S VOICE** serves family caregivers and professionals who work with adults with cognitive impairment or dementia caused by Alzheimer's, stroke, related illnesses, or trauma. www.thecaregiversvoice.com

Going Deeper

- **BEYOND SUFFERING: A CHRISTIAN VIEW ON DISABILITY MINISTRY** is a groundbreaking course from the Christian Institute on Disability that is transforming how Christians view God's plan for disability and suffering. Available as a certificate program or for college credit! www.joniandfriends.org/BYS/

The ***Beyond Suffering Bible*** is the first topical Bible written for those who suffer and the people who love them. Joni Eareckson Tada and the experts at Joni and Friends' Christian Institute on Disability provide uplifting insights that move us beyond the "why" of suffering. This Bible helps readers take hold of the eternal value God is building into our lives, especially as we find ourselves in the valleys of life. For more information visit www.beyondsufferingbible.com.

HARDCOVER 978-1-4143-9202-8
SOFTCOVER 978-1-4143-9558-6
BROWN/TAN DELUXE LEATHERLIKE 978-1-4143-9559-3
BROWN/TAN DELUXE LEATHERLIKE (indexed) 978-1-4143-9560-9
TEAL/BROWN/ROSE GOLD LEATHERLIKE 978-1-4143-9561-6
TEAL/BROWN/ROSE GOLD LEATHERLIKE (indexed) 978-1-4143-9562-3

- **NANCY REAGAN** described the process of losing her husband President Ronald Reagan to Alzheimer's as the "long goodbye." For over ten years she watched him slowly slip away from the loving, enduring friendship they shared for over five decades, leaving her with a handful of old love letters. After the President's death in 2004, Mrs. Reagan became a powerful advocate for finding a cure for Alzheimer's.[2]

Alzheimer's disease is the most common form of dementia and the sixth-leading cause of death in the United States. People with dementia experience a decline in their mental ability to carry out daily activities. In addition to Alzheimer's, other categories of dementia include Parkinson's disease, vascular dementia, Lewy bodies dementia, and Huntington's disease. Medicines are available to slow the progress of memory loss, but there is no cure at this time. Alzheimer's kills more people than breast cancer and prostate cancer combined.[3]

. Severe Alzheimer's Disease (late-stage)

- **THE DISEASE** progresses to increasingly physical implications: extreme weight loss, impaired walking and speaking, muscle rigidity, bladder and bowel issues.
- **FULL-TIME** supervision is required for simple daily activities (feeding, bathing, dressing, engaging with others, etc.).
- **OXYGEN LEVELS,** blood pressure, and skin condition must be monitored frequently, since infections such as urinary tract infection and pneumonia are often the cause of death in late-stage Alzheimer's.
- **WHILE THE PERSON** may seem to be incapable of communication, he or she can often still appreciate the loving touch and kind words of family and friends.

"I thought once I had made the decision to place my husband in a care home I would adjust to the new normal. But I felt a constant push/pull, wanting to visit him all the time. I became more, not less, depressed and started to withdraw. One day as I visited him, I broke down in uncontrollable sobs. As I covered my eyes, I felt a big hand cover mine. A quiet voice said, 'It's okay.' It was the same hand and voice that had encouraged me for most of my life. I was eventually able to enjoy friends again and trust God with our tomorrows."

—ANNA, WIFE OF CHARLES, WHO HAS HUNTINGTON'S DISEASE

MEMORIES ARE A LEGACY

DEBBIE VISITED HER DAD at a care home twice a week to feed him dinner. Three major strokes in 2011 had left her dad, a career U.S. Air Force colonel, with limited mental and physical abilities. One evening around the table the residents seemed more engaged than usual, as lively music from their era played in the background. As Debbie began wheeling her dad's chair around in time with the music, he grinned and nodded his head to the beat. She took his hands, swinging them to and fro. The caregiver noticed and offered to help him stand up so they could "dance" together. As he made it to his feet, one song ended and another started playing. Tears immediately welled up in Debbie's eyes as she recognized the tune. It was "Moon River"—the very song she had chosen for the father-daughter dance at her wedding so many years ago. *Would her dad remember?* Looking up at him, there was no doubt—he knew! Debbie rejoiced in this true blessing from God, and she will never forget her dad's legacy of love.

Even in the face of memory loss, we can help our friends create the memories that will be passed down from generation to generation. Your service to your friend is itself a legacy of faithful service, and when done "as though you were working for the Lord" (Colossians 3:23), it honors and brings glory to him as well.

WE ARE MORE THAN OUR MEMORIES

"AT SOME POINT, most caregivers admit that they feel absolutely alone, as if no one understands what they are going through."
—Dr. Benjamin Mast, from *Second Forgetting*[6]

There are 15 million unpaid caregivers in America supporting people with some form of memory loss—most are family members.[7] The demands of caring for a family member are often overwhelming, constantly changing, emotionally and financially draining, and require extreme patience and longsuffering. Yet many caregivers say their sacrifice is freely given out of a heart of love. Decisions are never easy, but the responsibility is an honor and blessing for many family members.

After 22 years as president of Columbia International University, Dr. Robertson McQuilkin retired to care for his wife, Muriel, who had Alzheimer's disease. "I have a theory that characteristics developed across the years come out at times like these," he says. "As I watch her brave descent into oblivion, Muriel is the joy of my life. Daily I discern new manifestations of the kind of person she is, the wife I always loved. I also see fresh manifestations of God's love—the God I long to love more fully."[8]

© 2016 Joni and Friends
Aspire Press, an imprint of
Rose Publishing, LLC
www.hendricksonrose.com

 020718SCG

Product code: 4166X

AspirePress

RELIGION/Christian Life/Personal Growth

ISBN 978-1-62862-477-9

Joni and Friends
INTERNATIONAL DISABILITY CENTER

9 781628 624779

Photos on pages 2, 3, 4 used with permission of Joni and Friends.

Retailers 5-pack 4170X ISBN: 9781628624830